Barefoot
BABY-PROOF

chomp-proof · rip-proof · water-proof

Big and Small

Britta Teckentrup

lion

cat

apple

seed

shark

fish

tree

acorn

sunflower

bee

bird

worm

mountain

snowflake

Why Barefoot Baby-Proof?

- Perfect for babies to explore with ALL their senses
- Created to meet a baby's developmental needs
- Opening the youngest hearts and minds

chomp-proof

rip-proof

water-proof

Small fingers point. Little mouths say.
What big and small things can you see today?

Let's learn first nature words together.

AGES 0+

Barefoot Books
23 Bradford Street, 2nd Floor, Concord, MA 01742
29/30 Fitzroy Square, London, W1T 6LQ
Illustrations copyright © 2013 by Britta Teckentrup
This Barefoot Baby-Proof edition first published in 2024
All rights reserved. Library of Congress Cataloging-in-Publication Data is available under 2012038494
Printed in Shenzhen, China. July 2024
3 5 7 9 8 6 4 2

Barefoot Baby-Proofs meet ASTM-F963 and CPSIA safety standard

Barefoot Books
step inside a story

www.barefootbooks.com

ISBN 979-8-88859-311-0

9 798888 593110 >